Contents

 Fiction

Excuses, Excuses
page 2

Written by
Alison Hawes
Illustrated by
Stephen Elford

Series editor **Dee Reid**

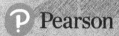

P Pearson

Characters

Sophie

Luka

Miss Smith

Sophie's mum

Tricky words

- excuse
- once
- hospital
- plaster

- difficult
- listened
- wailed
- tomorrow

Read these words to the student. Help them with these words when they appear in the text.

Introduction

Sophie went to Aspen Road School. One day she hadn't done her homework for Miss Smith. Luka told her to make up an excuse, so Sophie told Miss Smith that her mum had fallen and broken her arm. At first Miss Smith listened to Sophie's excuses but then she meets Sophie's mum.

Excuses, Excuses

Sophie hadn't done her homework for Miss Smith.
So she told Luka.
"Make up an excuse," he said, "I always do!"
"But I like Miss Smith," Sophie said. "I don't
want to lie."
"But it's only this once!" said Luka.

So Sophie told Miss Smith her mum had fallen and broken her arm.

"We had to wait at the hospital for it to be put into plaster," said Sophie, "so there was no time left for homework."

Luka saw Sophie later.
"What did you do?" he said.
"I made up an excuse," said Sophie, "it was easy!"

So when Sophie didn't do her homework the next week, she told Miss Smith she had to help her mum after school.

"It's difficult for Mum to do things with one arm," she said.
Miss Smith listened and said it was OK.

Then a week later, Miss Smith saw
Sophie and her mum in town.
Sophie's mum didn't have a plaster on her arm.
"I'm pleased to see your arm is better,"
said Miss Smith.

Sophie's mum laughed and said, "My arm is OK!
You must be thinking of someone else."
Sophie went very red.
But to her surprise, Miss Smith just said,
"Oh dear! I'm always getting things wrong!"

Sophie knew she was in trouble with Miss Smith.
So that night she made sure she did her homework.
She left it on the kitchen table so she wouldn't
forget it in the morning.

But in the morning, her homework wasn't there. "But I left it on the table!" wailed Sophie. "It must be here!"

"Oh no!" said Sophie's mum. "I took out the rubbish last night. Perhaps I threw out your homework too!"

Sophie tipped out the bin and looked for her homework.

She found her homework but it was wet and smelled of last night's chicken dinner.
But she had no time to do her homework again.
"It will have to do," said Sophie.

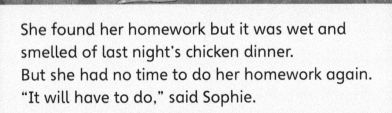

But Sophie tripped as she ran down Aspen Road.
Her homework fell out of her bag and
blew down the road.
A dog ran after it.
It liked the smell of the chicken dinner.

By the time Sophie got to the dog it had
eaten her homework.

Miss Smith told Sophie to stay behind after class. She wanted to know what her excuse was this time for not doing her homework.

"A dog ate my homework," said Sophie.
Miss Smith laughed. "Oh really?" she said.
"But a dog *did* eat my homework!" wailed Sophie.

"You must stay behind after school tomorrow," said Miss Smith. "You can do your homework then."
"But…" said Sophie.
"No buts!" said Miss Smith.
"But… It's Luka's birthday tomorrow and we're going bowling after school!" wailed Sophie.

But for once, Miss Smith really wasn't listening!

Quiz ////////////////////

Text comprehension

Literal comprehension

p10 Why did Sophie do her homework after Miss Smith had seen her mum?

p12 What happened to Sophie's homework?

Inferential comprehension

p6 Why did Sophie go on making up excuses?

p9 Why didn't Miss Smith challenge Sophie when she discovered her mum did not have a broken arm?

p15 Why did Miss Smith not believe Sophie about the dog eating her homework?

Personal response

- Have you ever made up an excuse for not doing your homework? Did you get away with it?
- Do you feel sorry for Sophie?

Word knowledge

p3 Find a word made up of two words.

p9 Find a word that starts with a silent letter.

p11 Find a word that means 'cried'.

Spelling challenge

Read these words:

does   gone   knew

Now try to spell them!

Ha! Ha! Ha!

Why did the boy eat his homework?

Because his teacher said it was a piece of cake!

Find out about

- how some people tell really big lies to become rich and famous.

Tricky words

- famous
- princess
- Russian
- murdered

- escaped
- believed
- Eiffel Tower
- lawyer

Read these words to the student. Help them with these words when they appear in the text

Introduction

People often tell lies to con people out of their money or they pretend to be somebody or something they are not, so they can become rich or famous. One woman pretended to be a princess from the Russian royal family but really she was a factory worker from Poland.

Really Big Lies

Some people tell really big lies to become rich.
Some people tell really big lies to become famous.
Some people tell really big lies to become both rich and famous!

Anna Anderson

This woman told a really big lie.
She said she was a princess from
the Russian royal family.
People thought that the whole family
had been murdered.
But then Anna said she was one of
the Russian princesses and she had escaped
when the rest of her family were murdered.

In 1918 the Russian royal family were murdered.

Lots of people believed her.
But some people thought it was odd
as Anna couldn't speak Russian!
But after she died, DNA tests proved
she was a factory worker from Poland,
not a Russian princess!

Victor Lustig

In 1925 this man told a really big lie!
He pretended that he owned the
Eiffel Tower!
Some people believed him.

Then he tried to sell the Eiffel Tower. He told a man to buy it for scrap metal. The man believed Victor owned it and was conned out of his money.

Han van Meergeren

In the 1930s this man began selling paintings. He said they were by famous artists.

But it was a lie!
He was painting them himself.
People found out, but he died before
he could be sent to prison.

Frank Abagnale

Frank became a conman in the 1960s
when he was only a teenager.
He told some big lies.
By the time he was 21, he had made
lots of money by pretending to be
a pilot, a doctor and a lawyer!

This is from a film made about Frank's life.

Frank did go to prison, but now
he helps to catch other conmen!

Janet Cooke

In 1980, this woman told a big lie.
She wrote a newspaper story about an
8 year old boy called Jimmy.
She said Jimmy was a drug addict.
She won a prize for her story.
But Jimmy wasn't real!
She had made him up for the prize money.
She lost her job and had to return the prize.

Rosie Ruiz

In 1980, this woman won the
Boston Marathon.
But it was a lie!
She had only run the last part of the race!
When she thought no one was looking she
joined in and pretended that she had been
running the whole race.

Milli Vanilli

Milli Vanilli were a pop group in the 1980s.
They were very popular.
Then it was found out that they were pretending
to sing along to the music!
All their records had been recorded by other singers.

Bernie Madoff

This man was a conman.
For years he conned thousands of people
into investing lots of money into his company.
But the company wasn't real and people lost
all their money.
In 2009, he was sent to
prison for 150 years!

Quiz /////////////

Text comprehension

Literal comprehension
p20 What big lie did Anna Anderson tell?
p29 How did Rosie Ruiz cheat in the Boston Marathon?

Inferential comprehension
p26 Why was a film made about Frank Abagnale's life?
p27 Why is Frank used to help catch other conmen?
p30 Why did Milli Vanilli only pretend to sing?

Personal response
- Do you think you would have been tricked by any of these conmen?
- How would you feel if you had been tricked by a conman?

Word knowledge

p23 Find a word that means 'tricked'.
p28 Find a word made up of two words.
p31 Why is there an exclamation mark after '150 years!'?

Spelling challenge

Read these words:

other   year   quick

Now try to spell them!

Ha! Ha! Ha!

What do you call two robbers?

A pair of knickers!